John Farman

THE SHORT AND BLOODY HISTORY OF KNIGHTS

Red Fox

Random House Children's Books
61-63 Uxbridge Road, London W5 5SA

A division of The Random House Group Ltd
London Melbourne Sydney Auckland
Johannesburg and agencies throughout the world

3 5 7 9 10 8 6 4 2

First published in Great Britain by
Red Fox Children's Books 2000

Printed and bound in Denmark by
Nørhaven Paperback, Viborg

Papers used by Random House Group Ltd are natural,
recyclable products made from wood grown in sustainable forests.
The manufacturing processes conform to the
environmental regulations of the country of origins.

The Random House Group Limited Reg. No. 954009

www.kidsatrandomhouse.co.uk

ISBN 0 09 940712 4

CONTENTS

WHAT IS A KNIGHT?

'Knight: . . . one of gentle birth, bred to arms, admitted in feudal
times to a certain honourable military rank . . .'
Chambers Dictionary

Everyone thinks they know about knights: rich guys in flash
armour tearing around the countryside, culling excess
dragons, rescuing damsels trapped in towers and knocking
each other off horses with long poles at special tournaments!

So why write yet another book, I expect you're
wondering? Simple! I wanted to find out all the stuff we
don't know. Like, where did knights buy their armour? How
much did it cost? How easy was it to run about, let alone
fight, covered from head to foot in metal? What did they get
paid for fighting for the King? What did they eat? Where
did they live – and with whom? Were they really the brave,

noble fellows we are led to believe, or were some weedy, cowardly and dishonest? In this book I'm going to try to tell you what knights were really like and what it was like to be one – warts and all.

Career Knights

The first thing to remember is that knights were the very first mercenaries. They were paid, usually with large plots of land, to fight for their lord or king.

The second thing to remember is that they were supposed to conduct themselves according to a strict code of behaviour. This was called *chivalry* and I'll deal with that in the next chapter.

Lastly, and most importantly, the knights were part of a whole way of life, called the feudal system, that came over from Europe. Basically the feudal system was a way for a king to raise the thousands of men needed for the wars he was always fighting. His top barons and earls, in exchange for vast areas of land, would pledge to provide armies on request. These barons and earls would then give smaller parcels of their land to knights who, in return, promised to provide the actual guys to do the dirty work. In return for doing this, the knight would give these peasants much smaller bits of land to provide food for their families – and the knight's family. All jolly unfair.

How to be a Knight

But who got to be a knight? For a start, before you get too excited, you had to be the son of a knight to start with. At about twelve you'd be sent to another knight's house to learn how to do it – so to speak. The knight in question would use you simply as a page to start with and then as a personal servant called a *squire*. This would involve grooming

his horses, polishing his armour and even serving him with his breakfast, tea★ and supper. In return you'd be taught how to ride horses and fight at the same time, as well as learn the art of chivalry as mentioned above.

Knight Time

Eventually when the knight in charge of you reckoned you were ready, it would be time for the big day. First this would involve a special bath in holy water with prayers and stuff. Then you'd have to put on an outfit of white clothes and pray all night in front of your nice new armour that would have been put on the altar. Just like Christmas, you weren't allowed to touch it until morning. Once all your rellies and friends had arrived at the church you could put your armour on while the priest blessed it with you inside. That done, another knight would give you a whack on the shoulder with the flat (hopefully) of his sword and, hey presto, you were a fully-fledged knight.

★ *Tea (the drink) didn't actually come to Europe till the eighteenth century, but you know what I mean.*

EARLY KNIGHTS

We British always like to think that knights were our invention – Sir Galahad, Sir Lancelot and all those other guys who hung around the Round Table. But, much to my dismay, I must break the news that it looks very much as if knights were a German idea. Even the very word knight comes from the German *knecht*. Bad news eh!

In the Middle Ages, France was occupied by a bunch of German-speaking tribes called the Franks. Now we all know how much the Germans like taking over other people's countries without even asking (see First and Second World Wars), and these prototype Germans were no exception.

When the Roman Empire began to decline and fall, these Franks, under Clovis I, took advantage and by AD 494 all of northern France was under their control. Then Clovis got religion and decided to become a Catholic. He then insisted that all the Franks became Catholic too, which united all the various Frankish tribes into one people.

So what's all this got to do with knights? Please be patient.

The Muslims had been slowly building a massive empire – by the eighth century Egypt, Palestine, Syria, Persia and North Africa had all fallen to their armies. But these ruling Arabs, not content with running half the known world, wanted the other half too and even the bits that weren't known – as soon as they were (if you see what I mean). Then in 711 the massive Muslim army hit Spain and the soldiers were sunning themselves on the beaches of the South of France by the following year. Something had to be done to prevent the Muslims taking all of western Europe and it fell to the Franks, who had the most powerful medieval kingdom, to do it.

Charles Martel in France, our King Alfred in England and a German called Henry the Fowler provided loads of horses to help repel the raiders. The new cavalry were the first to use stirrups, which enabled them to gallop much faster (without crippling themselves in very embarrassing places). So in 716 the Muslims were stopped in their tracks as they swept into mainland France, by the cavalry of Charles Martel, the Franks' leader.

But war-horses were expensive and learning how to use them properly took years of training. To support his cavalry, the now ever-so-popular Martel gave his top soldiers lumps of land, which he snatched from the Church. These were to be farmed by dependent peasants. This was just the very beginning of feudalism. The only condition was that these soldiers would fight for him, no questions asked, equipped with their own horses and any weapons they might need.

During the latter half of the eighth century, the mighty and dead famous Charlemagne doubled the Frankish kingdom, continually pushing back the now mega-miffed Muslims wherever he came across them.

But what has this got to do with knights?

Well, it was Charlemagne's world famous cavalry, taken from the most noble of Frankish families, who were the very first proper knights, so making knighthood a military rank. Being rich, it was no problem for these chaps to supply their own horses, chainmail shirts, helmets, swords, clothes and all the other stuff required to fight wars – right down to enough packed lunches to last up to three months at a time. These lads made the most savage, cruel, efficient and formidable army that you could ever have had the misfortune to bump into.

Knight's Service

It was from this Frankish kingdom that the proper feudal system, which was to take over the whole of the western world, developed. As I explained briefly before, it worked like this.

Every scrap of land in those days belonged to the sovereign prince – be he king, duke, marquis or count (he told everyone that he'd been given it by God, by the way). This prince then issued *fiefs*, land given in return for military service, to his barons. The barons in turn gave bits of their fiefs to knights (or vassals) who pledged to fight for them and, therefore, the sovereign prince. This land would have to support fifteen to thirty peasant families who were not allowed to go and work or do much else come to that – anywhere else! The soldiers, taken from these families, would also have to be prepared to fight whoever and wherever their master was asked to go and also to guard the big boss's castle if it was under attack. All in all they would expect to spend at least forty days a year in his lordship's service – for nothing.

What all this actually meant was that throughout Europe, at the drop of his crown, the King or even a lord could raise a huge army of admittedly not-always-very-good soldiers to go fight whomever he pleased.

Brotherhood

So it was through this feudalism business, which spread right the way through Europe, that these knights felt a sort of brotherhood with their foreign counterparts. By the eleventh century knighthood in Europe had become hereditary (passed down from father to son), provided the new boy accepted the same responsibilities as his dad to their overlord.

Dub Dub

Knights from the eleventh century onwards had to be *dubbed* at special ceremonies (swords on shoulders etc.), where they would swear an oath to defend the Church and protect the womenfolk, widows, orphans and pets as well as the sick and old. The swearing bit was easy, as it turned out, but it became increasingly clear that many knights simply showed two fingers to the Church. They used their muscle to rob the poor, take advantage of the women (if you get my meaning) and live in luxury at the expense of everyone else.

I DUB YOU SIR - WHOOPS!

Knights' Rules OK

The whole idea of how a knight was supposed to behave went under the general term of 'chivalry'. Chivalry comes from the old French word for soldiers on horses – *chevalerie*. This is because hereditary knights arrived in Britain with the French-speaking Normans in 1066. Every knight was supposed to be bound by the rules of chivalry which were as follows:

1   A knight should never tell porkies.
2   He must defend the Holy Church (which in those days was headed by the Pope in Italy).
3   He should defend the weak, suppress the wicked and honour God with noble acts (juggling? acrobatics?).
4   He must be brave and loyal in defence of the knight who knighted him – and his lady.
5   Women (by that, read 'posh women') must be held in high regard, even though they have no legal rights or power.
6   A knight should on no account have it off with another knight's girl.
7   The object in battle should always be to capture the enemy not kill him.
8   Knights must never fight during Lent and should even get a couple of days off at Christmas.
9   If a nobleman is captured, he has to be treated according to his rank.

For Instance

When, in 1356, the Black Prince captured the King of France, John II, at Poitiers, he actually served him at his table and kept him in the most luxurious prison the Tower of London could offer.

To quote Chaucer's *The Canterbury Tales* from the mid-fourteeenth century: a knight was 'meeke as is a mayde. / He nevere yet no vileynye ne sayde / In al his lyf unto no maner wight'.

Sorry if you can't read ye olde English.

How to Build a Feudal Army

First of all, if a king knew that he had to get an army together for a specific battle, his first job would be to decide how many soldiers he might need (give or take a hundred). On the principle that you don't need a sledgehammer to crack a walnut, there was no point calling in 5,000 men to quell a punch-up in a tavern. Therefore, he would put the word out to all his earls and lords who would be expected to supply men in proportion to their quota (which depended on how much land they'd been given in the first place). Clear so far?

The earl would then call on all the knights that he in turn had given land (fiefs) to and tell them how many men he needed. If there was a good supply of soldiers, many of these knights preferred to pay *scutage*, a system by which they could buy their way out if they didn't fancy fighting. This was good for the king cos it meant he could buy the services of professional soldiers who were much better at fighting! This was the beginning of armies as we know them today. Earls, by the way, couldn't buy their way out as it was seen as their duty to turn up (unless too old, too young, too feeble or too mad). If the battle or siege went on for more than the initial (free) forty days, the king would be expected to pay the knights and soldiers proper wages. Earls, naturally, were expected to do it for nothing.

So you'd get a situation like they had in the wars of 1294 between Edward I and the Welsh rebels, where the Earl of Lancaster, who was lord over 263 knightly fiefs, turned up to fight for the King with only fifty men. The Earl of Norfolk, who also had 263 fiefs, pitched up with only twenty-eight and the greatest baron of Devon, Hugh Courtney, with ninety-two fiefs, only managed twelve – and so on and so on. This meant that the King received quite a lot of the old scutage money from those who preferred to pay-up rather than go to war. This wasn't a problem as it meant he could distribute all the extra cash to the many knights who'd showed up with far more than their fair share of soldiers.

In the case of these Welsh wars, the campaign continued well over the forty days, which meant that the King ran out of the old scutage money fairly quickly. This is where being able to jack up the taxation of the whole population at the drop of a hat, becomes so convenient. Anyway, it all worked out just fine in the end (providing you weren't Welsh) as Edward was able to keep his troops clothed and fed while the rebels (with tongue-twister names like Rhys-ap-Maredudd) eventually ended up starving in the hills. Once he'd beaten them, the King built a load of castles (like Conway) to house soldiers in safety while keeping the poor Welsh under their thumbs.

Big Rewards

Most wars were highly profitable for knights and barons alike. If you could capture your French counterpart during the wars of the fourteenth century, the chances are you could sell him back to his own side for huge amounts of hard cash. So huge that whole castles were built with the dosh. Their ladies too got lucky. There wasn't a large house in England that didn't have French silverware, furs and linen and the ladies themselves often wore beautiful clothes taken from the continent.

By the Way

Have you ever heard the term 'camp follower'? It comes from the small band of civilians that would follow an army to the battlefield in order to sell them food and wine. They could often be seen after all the fun was over, going amongst the stiffs, especially the dead knights, pinching any jewellery or valuables they could find. Rotten job, but somebody had to do it.

YIPPEE! GOLD TEETH

KNIGHTS AND GOD

Religion in the Middle Ages had its hands in just about
everything right up to its elbows.

It's quite important to realise that those who went into
the higher ranks of the Church came from the same stratum
of society as the knights – usually the better off landowners.
The Church, by the way, was a perfectly good alternative for
the landed gentry's sons and also their daughters
(especially the ones they couldn't marry off).
Very often a knight could call on his brother
in the Church to help him out in some
form or other and vice versa. If you go into
any really old church in England, you can
still see from the stained-glass windows and
all those lying-down statues of knights and
their wives just how important they
were in those days.

God Rules OK

God was everywhere in medieval England. Although there
was only a fraction of the buildings we see these days, there
were even more churches, chapels and monasteries. The very
rich knights often supported the church – paying for a new
spire here, or a new roof there – in return for flash family
tombs or their pictures on the church walls.

But despite living together fairly well, the Church, as I
suggested earlier, began to get more and more fed up with
the eternal arguments that often led to proper wars between
rival knights. They'd had enough of raiding parties of armed
'robber barons' tearing through their villages, burning the
monasteries, running off with their livestock and killing

anyone who seemed to have a problem with it. They were also a bit miffed with those overlords holed up in massive fortified castles who bled the surrounding countryside dry. At one stage the Catholic Church tried to make the warring knights agree to a *Truce of God*, threatening to excommunicate anyone that wouldn't play. Then, in 1041, at the Council of Nice, they went even further by forbidding wars on Sundays. Fine from Mondays through to Saturdays, but not Sundays. This was later extended to the period between Thursdays and Sundays inclusive, which is all a bit loony when you come to think of it. The knights, bless 'em, saw all this not only as a right swiz, but as an interference in their business. Most of them would have none of it.

HANG ON, MATE — IT'S ONLY SUNDAY

In 1077, Pope Gregory VII, head Catholic, put his big ecclesiastical boot right in it, ordering that everyone from peasant to king had to do as he said. The knights particularly, he said, were bound to obey whatever the Church told them – or else! Then Gregory, who was apparently a real tough guy, decided it was time to lead a Christian army against the non-Christians of the world, particularly the Muslims whom he reckoned were God's worst enemy. He vowed to relieve Jerusalem, which had been taken over from the Christian Byzantines, from Muslim clutches as soon as poss. This, in case you hadn't guessed, was when the Crusades all began. Pope Gregory had heard, through the grapevine, that Christian pilgrims, who were on their way to the Holy Land to worship, were being captured and sold as slaves, which was a bit of a blinking cheek even then.

Pilgrims

Although most people in the Middle Ages hardly knew what went on outside their villages (let alone in the rest of the world), there had been a constant stream of European Christian pilgrims travelling to and from the Holy Land, particularly Jerusalem. Once there, they would fall down in front of macabre holy relics – like splinters of wood from the cross, the tongue of St Mark, Jesus' crown of thorns, hair from the head of John the Baptist or the nails that went through their Lord's hands and feet etc.

Unfortunately Pope Gregory VII died in 1085, so it was down to his replacement Pope Urban II to continue Gregory's fight against the Muslims. When the Byzantine★ Emperor, Alexius, who'd lost so many provinces to the Muslims, wrote a remarkable letter to Pope Urban and a load of top lords, asking them to get armies together to help him, the Crusades began. In the letter, he described some of the ghastly atrocities committed by the Muslims. He talked

★ *The Byzantine Empire was formed from the eastern bit of the Roman Empire and ended in 1453.*

about young Christians being forced to pee in the font. Any
that refused were tortured to death. Some of the things they
did to the grown-up Christians were too frightful for even
me to describe (and that's pretty frightful, believe me).

Just to sweeten the pill, however, Alexius also happened
to mention that if saving Christians from their terrible fate
and rescuing Jerusalem from the infidels wasn't quite enough
for the Crusaders, there were enough fabulous treasures and
beautiful women to go round. They were there just for the
taking.

It worked a treat. The knights saw immediately that they
could not only satisfy a whinging Church that was
continually giving them grief, but also make loads of money
and meet tons of pretty dusky maidens – all by going and
fighting a Holy War. Brilliant stuff!

ANYONE FOR A CRUSADE?

In the last chapter I mentioned how the Muslims were becoming more and more powerful in the East, and about the nasty habit they had of trying to make everyone else think like they did (that's religion for you). The Crusaders, who were Christians, didn't like this at all (because they wanted everyone to think the same way as them). So in 1095 Pope Urban realised that it was time to stop whining and whinging about the Muslim infidels and do something about it. This is how the whole idea of the Crusades came about.

By the Way
You'll see the term infidel, meaning one who has no faith, used to describe the Muslims. The joke is that the Christians stole the term from the Muslims who first used it to describe them.

The First Crusade

You could say that the first Crusade kicked off at about
3.35p.m. on Tuesday, 27th November 1095 from a great big
field just outside the walls of the French city of Clermont-
Ferrand (the cathedral wasn't big enough to hold everyone).
The furious Pope yelled at the massed crowds that enough
was enough. The Turks were ever-encroaching into Christian
lands, ruining the churches and torturing the pilgrims. They
had now reached Jerusalem, the most precious jewel in the
Christian crown, and were daring to trash the most holy
places known to civilised man. It was time to teach those
Muslims not to mess with the Christians – the sword must
go into partnership with religion, he cried.

The response was so wildly enthusiastic that, at the end
of the meeting, all the 300 assembled bishops rushed back to
where they had come from to recruit as many Crusaders as
they could muster. Knights were actually ordained by the
Church and told they were on active service for the defence
of the only true faith, so much so that they actually began to
believe that by going to rescue Jerusalem they were working
for the old man (God) himself. The groups they raised were
to make their own way, at their own expense, to the
Byzantine city of Constantinople (now Istanbul, Turkey)
where they'd all meet up and together sally forth to attack
the Turks and anyone else who needed a good seeing to.

Once they'd done that and got the natives safely back
under the Christian thumb they'd go on to the main
business, which was dealing with the rest of the Muslims in
Palestine and Syria. Finally it would be onward Christian
soldiers, to snatch back the city of Jerusalem.

God and Money

We know from that famous letter of Pope Urban that there

was more on offer to knights fighting the Crusades than teaching the Muslim infidels a lesson, doing our god (God) a favour, or earning themselves eternal salvation and a nice little corner in heaven. Sure all these things and the fame that they would bring back home were pretty attractive, but on their own they weren't appealing enough to make people trudge through disease-ridden countries for months on end, only to run the risk of being terminated in ways they couldn't even dream of when they got to wherever it was they were going? Anyway, who was going to look after things back home – the farmlands, the serfs and, much more to the point, the wife.

No, there had to be more to it than that.

By the Way

It was for this reason that the notorious 'chastity belt' was invented. The lady of the house would have to be locked into a special device to stop her getting into any knightly frolics (at night) while the old man was away. Please don't try this at home!

Land Ahoy

You see, apart from the treasure and the babes, the Crusaders were also able to claim huge tracts of land and make fortunes by opening up trade routes from the cities that were about to be un-Muslimised. Cities like Venice, Genoa and Pisa.

By the Way

In a book, Geoffroi de Vigios describes the fantastic wealth of some knights after the Crusades. One, apparently just for a laugh, ploughed the land surrounding his castle and filled the furrows with silver coins just to make them glitter;

another had thirty horses burnt alive for a bet (beats racing, I suppose). Yet another cooked a massive banquet over millions of candles just to prove it was possible.

Crusading for All

In 1096 five huge armies of knights and noblemen set off, mostly from France and Germany but some from southern Italy. Alongside the noblemen travelled well over 20,000 ordinary people. 'All the common people, the chaste as well as the sinful, homicides, thieves, perjurers and robbers ... all joyfully entered upon the expedition' led by a middle-aged weirdo – a French priest called Peter the Hermit. They all gave up everything (which on the whole was not that much) to join the holy campaign and set out to walk over 2,000 miles to Jerusalem on what was later referred to as the Popular or Peasant Crusade.

By the Way

Peter the Hermit, though filthy to look at, was regarded as almost divine, so much so that the adoring throngs stole hairs from his donkey (soon bald) who apparently looked and smelt like his master, to be kept as religious relics.

VERY FUNNY

Roast Turkey

As the peasant Crusaders passed through Germany and on through Hungary and the Balkans they were joined by thousands more like-minded peasants who'd all been whipped up into religious fervour by their leaders. All-in-all, the peasant army travelling east could have been as many as 50,000. But religious Crusades are funny things. These so-called committed Christians thought nothing of robbing and looting Turkish Christians whom they passed on their way. There were even reports that the French contingent barbecued little baby Turks on spits when they got a bit peckish (the French always did have weird taste food-wise).

They had turned into an unruly, always-hungry mob, pillaging practically any town they came across – friendly or otherwise. It had become clear that most of the Peasant Crusaders had gone on the journey because it seemed a better option than staying behind and starving.

Bed and Who's Breakfast?

Mind you, they had to travel through other famine-struck regions to get there. It was reported that, while trudging across some remote bits of France and Germany, it was not unusual for the peasant Crusaders to put up at an inn only to have their throats cut and then be eaten by the locals.

Turkish Delight

In 1097 a bunch of Flemish peasant soldiers called Tafurs who travelled out to the East with Peter the Hermit, found themselves with the main 100,000 strong Crusaders' army attacking the almost unattackable city of Antioch (Syria). Owing to the size of the army, most of these Crusaders were starving in the arid, unyielding landscape. All except the Tafurs, who simply collected the carcasses of the dead Turks, cooked them up and ate them. When they began to run out of dead ones, they hunted live ones purely for the pot.

HOW'S YER TURK?

Anyone for Blood?

But the going was getting tough for the Crusaders wherever they were. At one stage 6,000 German and Italian Crusaders captured a castle called Xerigordon. The enemy Sultan promptly surrounded it and cut off its only water supply. After a few days in the blazing heat, the crazed Crusaders were so thirsty they emptied the blood out of their own horses and asses and drank it. After eight days they gave in and the pesky Muslims slaughtered anyone who wouldn't renounce Christianity. I think I just might have lied.

Later, at another deserted fortress at Civeton, on the Bosporus, the occupying Crusaders, who formed the large part of Peter the Hermit's enormous peasant army, marched out to meet the Turks who were preparing to attack. Unfortunately, they walked straight into an ambush and were forced to scurry back to the fortress with the Turkish infidels hot on their heels. A few thousand escaped, but the rest of the fleeing soldiers, as well as all the women and children within the walls, were hacked to death and all that was left was a mountain of bones. Later, when rebuilding the fortress walls, the Turks used these bones like pebbles to fill up the cracks in the huge stones. (Waste not want not, I expect they thought.) It still stands today as a sort of tomb to the dead Crusaders.

NOW WHAT CAN WE FILL THOSE CRACKS WITH?

Peter was not killed, as he had been away negotiating

with the Emperor Alexius. But most of his army was destroyed and the whole Peasant's Crusade all turned a bit sad as very few of these hopelessly ill-equipped common folk ever reached the Middle East. The ones who did were so bad at fighting they were made mincemeat of by the fearsome Muslims. Practically none saw the eventual Christian takeover of Jerusalem in 1099.

The nobleman army, made up of proper knights on the other hand, had it a little easier, sweeping through to Constantinople like a dose of salts. In 1097 it was on to their first major target of Nicaea, the Anatolian Turkish capital.

Siege of Nicaea

Every Crusader had to cross the Bosporus at some time or another, as it divided the narrow land between the Mediterranean and Black Seas. In order to move on they felt they had to capture the mighty city of Nicaea (Iznik these days). But the city was heavily fortified and protected by a hundred towers. It was, therefore, almost impregnable. The Crusaders besieged the city for two weeks, but the Turks inside weren't giving in that easily. Their boss, the Sultan Kilij Arslan, was away with most of his army fighting some rival Muslims at the time (they were all at it in those days) but came back every now and again to try to besiege the besiegers.

The Nicaean Turks' favourite trick, when bored with firing their bows and arrows, was to lower iron hooks over the massive walls and try to hoik up the bodies of the dead or wounded Crusaders that lay at the bottom – a bit like hooking plastic ducks at the fair. If they succeeded, they'd whip them up to the top, strip them of their armour and fling the naked carcasses back at their enemies below. The

Crusaders, not to be outdone, chopped off the heads of the Turkish corpses and prisoners and catapulted them back over the walls. *Touché*!

The occupants of Nicaea refused to submit as they were still getting supplies by boat across Lake Ascania. But the Byzantine navy eventually turned up and put a stop to that. The head Turk, realising the game was nearly up, then made an agreement with the Byzantine admiral that they could have the city as long as they didn't harm anyone. This really annoyed the rest of the Crusaders, who'd been looking forward to a good slaughter, but strangely enough they kept their word.

After many similar battles and sieges, the brave all-conquering Crusaders eventually reached Jerusalem (in 1099) which was under Egyptian control. After a short but ever so bloody siege they lost patience and jumped over the walls, massacring just about everyone inside. Then they all went home, leaving a Frankish Duke called Godfrey de Bouillon in charge.

The Second Crusade

Once in charge, Godfrey promptly established four Christian states, the most powerful being the State of Jerusalem (which was in a real state after all that fighting). But the Muslims were hopping mad and certainly weren't going to lie down and take it. Gradually regrouping they formed a massive army and under a new leader, Imad ed-Din Zangi they hit back by taking the state of Edessa in 1144. This was important as it had been the first Crusader kingdom to be created.

The Pope of the day would have none of it and begged the new generation of knights to get out their swords and have another go. This time the rallying call attracted even more recruits owing to the success of the last campaign. The army even included the Holy Roman Emperor Conrad II who led a German army from Nuremberg in 1147. The French force left a little later but both armies were severely ambushed on the way by the tricksy Muslims, and although a few reached Jerusalem, most went home.

This cheered the Muslims up no end and left them free to regroup. By 1169, under the mighty Saladin (see page 74) they were ready to get back the lands they had lost. This time they surrounded Jerusalem on three sides and, after much to-ing and fro-ing, Saladin's massive army overran the whole kingdom. All the knights who had remained were beheaded to teach them a lesson (which it probably did!).

The Third Crusade

Back home in Europe everyone was furious and very soon, in 1191, a third Crusade was on its way to get Saladin and his bully boys. This time the Holy Roman Emperor, Frederick I, French king Philip II and our very own Richard I were part of the largest Crusader army ever seen. Unfortunately Frederick died on the way and most of his army sloped home to Germany while the other two kings failed to capture Jerusalem – or anything else – back from Saladin.

The Fourth and Fifth Crusades

The next two Crusades were rather weedy affairs. The fourth in 1202 only managed to capture and plunder Constantinople, and the fifth achieved absolutely nothing and ended with the Christian army putting up its hands and running home.

Early Knights

Now this is where the whole thing gets really weird. In 1212, thousands of French and German kids, disgusted at the knights' lack of success in getting the Holy Land back off the infidels, decided to have a go themselves and in so doing hopefully become true Knights of the Cross. Would you fancy doing that?

In France the mini-Crusade was led by a fast-talking twelve-year-old shepherd boy called Stephen who promised them that when they got to the seaside the sea would dry up before them, like it had for Moses, and a sign would be uncovered saying 'Jerusalem this Way' (honest!). There'd be no need for boats to make the first bit of the journey to the Holy Land.

Thirty thousand children under twelve set off from Vendôme behind this medieval Pied Piper but by the time they got to the sea at Marseilles many had dropped out exhausted by the severe July heat.

Anyway, they waited and waited but, guess what, the sea stayed as wet and as deep as ever. Eventually a couple of rich merchants took pity on the poor children and hired seven ships to take them to the Holy Land. The poor little misguided beggars were never heard of again. Well, not for twenty years, when the true story emerged. Two of the ships had gone down in a storm with all hands, and the rest of the children were surrounded by the dreaded Saracens almost as soon as they stepped off the blinking boats and promptly sold as slaves to Muslim traders. The tip-off had apparently come from those two merchants in Marseilles.

The Last Crusades

Frederick II, the new Holy Roman Emperor, thought he'd go it alone in 1215 but never actually managed to get it together until 1227. The poor old guy hadn't got very far out of port before he fell sick and had to go back home,

leaving his army. The Pope, who'd been waiting impatiently for the Crusade to kick off, lost his cool altogether and, showing a severe lack of sympathy, excommunicated the poor, sick Emperor (which meant he couldn't be a Christian any more). This didn't stop our Freddie, however, for in 1228, when feeling better, he set off again to find his army. When he got to where he thought they'd be – they weren't. Apparently most of them had got fed up waiting and had done a runner. He therefore did a deal with the Egyptian Sultan al-Kamil and succeeded in getting the kingdom of Jerusalem back for the Crusaders. Despite this, he was still shunned by the Pope, believe it or not, and the ungrateful so-and-so even sent a little Crusade to try to nick Frederick's Italian possessions while he was away.

After a couple more small Crusades, the last one left in 1270, when Louis IX set off with his knights to capture the city of Tunis. This ended when the king died of something rather unpleasant in Tunisia (as you so often did) during the summer of 1270. There were further attempts to try and raise Crusades but, quite frankly, everyone was so fed up with continually sailing across treacherous seas, climbing over torturous mountain passes and trekking across searing deserts (before having to face the dreaded foe), that they began to hesitate. In the end, all that was left as a result of the whole blinking business were a load of dusty old Crusader churches, a few battered old castles and a history full of tall stories.

FOREIGN KNIGHTS

You might have heard people talk about the Knights
Templars or the Knights Hospitallers. In this chapter I'll try
to explain what they were all about with a few of the other
knighty types thrown in for good
measure.

The Knights Templars

These were a rather splendid
bunch of knights who were
something between things
godly and things military and
were recognised wherever
they went by their brilliant
white tabards sporting big
red crosses.

By the Way

The crosses worn by the Templars were Maltese crosses, not
quite the same as the Christian crosses worn by Richard the
Lionheart (on his cloak), or the Crusaders (over their
breastplates).

They began as a little gang of eight knights led by the
Burgundian knight Hugh de Payens and his mate Andre de
Montbard. They acted as guides and protectors to the
Christian pilgrims passing through hostile lands on their way
to Jerusalem. Up until the middle of the eleventh century,
the Muslims, who held Jerusalem, had allowed Christian
pilgrims to visit. When a different bunch of Muslims
(Turkish ones) took over, they went out of their way to

attack and rob the pilgrims on the way there, regarding them as a gift from God ... and then stopped them coming altogether. This made the knights very cross indeed.

By the time the first Crusade was well under way, these chaps decided to become a religious order, calling themselves The Poor Knights of the Temple of Solomon or the Knights Templars for short. They were first recognised by the Church at the Council of Troyes (and given permission to wear their famous red crosses) by Bernard of Clairvaux. He did so well, by the way, that he went on to be a saint. Bernard was the most important churchman of the time and rather liked the idea of knights who were religious rather than just out for what they could get. He granted them their rule (called *The Rule*) in 1128. Gifts and support poured in and soon most major cities had recruitment centres where the starter-knights from the best families in Europe went to be trained.

Sworn to a life of poverty, chastity and obedience, they became the most dedicated and scary soldiers and would fight anywhere they were required. They became so powerful that eventually they chose which of the king's orders they would obey. At their height, there were 20,000 Knights Templars as well as their sergeants, chaplains and servants. They owned massive estates from Denmark and the Orkney Islands in the north, to Italy and Spain in the south.

The Knights Templars became most famous for defending the Christian enclave of Jerusalem in the Holy Land even though they did fall out big-time with their rivals the Knights Hospitallers (coming next). To say 'fall out' was no exaggeration – they hated each other with a passion. In the end they were fighting each other in the streets.

After the Crusades most of the ordinary Crusaders went home, so the job of keeping the Turks and Egyptians at bay fell to the Templars and Hospitallers. This was where all those mighty Crusader castles came from, that stretch all the way through Turkey and Southern Europe. Because they actually lived in the Holy Land, the Templars often looked at things differently from the part-time Crusaders who, let's face it, only turned up for short periods to fight the Muslims and grab as much money as they could get their hands on.

After the capture of Acre in 1291 the last bit of the kingdom of Jerusalem was lost and the Templars withdrew to their European operations. These involved international trade, banking and diplomacy at which they were so brilliant that they soon became ludicrously wealthy (so much for their vows of poverty). They even had a huge fleet of highly manoeuvrable war ships (fitted with battering rams) so that they could carry pilgrims and troops with their horses. They had been able to make their huge profits partly due to the fact that they had long ago been given exemption from taxes. Also, they didn't have to answer to any law but God's (which was a bit of a swiz for everyone else). As is usually the case, this made them very unpopular.

By the Way

Did you know that the Knights Templars were responsible for bringing the idea of mouth to mouth resuscitation, the telescope and the 'note of hand' (personal cheque) to Europe from the Holy Land? The long distance traveller could carry a kind of Templars' credit card which not only saved him carrying cash, but meant that he could use it wherever there was a Templar in residence.

So the Knights Templars became richer and richer and more and more powerful until, in October 1307 (Friday 13th)★, King Philip of France, who was getting exceedingly hot under the crown, hit on the idea of accusing them of heresy (disagreeing with the teachings of the Church).

★ *Unlucky for some.*

This showed a certain amount of sour grapes as he'd been refused admission to the order when a young man. All the Knights Templars in France were arrested and the order was promptly abolished. The knights were then tortured so badly that they admitted to a whole bunch of crimes they didn't do – like peeing on the crucifix, for which they were burnt slowly. The Templars' property was then handed over to the Hospitallers who were waiting in the wings with huge grins on their faces. The Pope then ordered that similar persecution of the Templars should happen in every country in which the Templars owned property.

By the Way

It is thought that seventeen Templar ships, loaded with all the immense hoard of treasure that had been stored in Paris Temple 29, left various French ports. The treasure was never seen again. If you want to know where it is, send me a fiver and I'll tell you.★

★ *Oh no, you won't: Ed.*

The Knights of St John of Jerusalem – or the Knights Hospitallers

These were the other great order of religious knights who gradually got more and more into fighting for a living. Their main job had also been to guard, guide and comfort the weary and sick pilgrims on their way to and from the Holy Sepulchre in Jerusalem. In 1112 their monastery (or hospital) not only held all of them, but up to 2,000 guests (sounds more like a hotel than a hospital!). These guys wore black outfits with white crosses and also built fab castles which became hospitals for old or sick knights as well as barracks for their soldiers.

Psst!

How do you make a Maltese cross?
Punch him in the mouth!

Acre fell to the Muslims in 1291 so the Hospitallers settled in Cyprus to regroup and then went into the profitable shipping business, providing all the Christian countries with supplies from the East while keeping down pirates in the Mediterranean. In 1307 they bought the now-Greek island of Rhodes and made it their fortified headquarters (you can still see their castles on the island). But the Muslims didn't like having a Christian stronghold so close to their lands and attacked them (unsuccessfully) in 1435.

After the sacking of Constantinople in 1453 by the Turks, the Hospitallers became the last Christians in the whole of the East which made life even dodgier for them. They were set upon several times again and were finally beaten in 1522 when the massive army of Suleiman the Magnificent let them leave the island with their lives as a mark of respect for their almost loony bravery.

Emperor Charles V who thought they were dead cool, promptly gave them the island of Malta, which was a good deal all considered. Blow me if that blasted Suleiman (now seventy) didn't have another go. The amazing Knights Hospitallers with only 700 knights and 1,500 men would have none of it and managed to hold off the full might of the Turkish Empire and became legendary heroes for their trouble.

By the Way

The Knights Hospitallers, established in 1100 in England, survived until 1540 when Henry VIII put them out. Queen Victoria, for some reason, re-instated them in 1888.
The Knights Templars and the Knights Hospitallers still exist, but only as social clubs (just like the Freemasons) patronised by businessmen.

Teutonic Knights of the Virgin Mary

Yet another bunch of religious knuts – sorry – knights, who
followed vows of poverty, chastity and obedience. This lot
were set up after the fall of Acre, Germany, and were only
concerned with protecting German pilgrims. They were
known by their white tunic with a black cross (confusing or
what?). In the thirteenth century they switched from
protecting people to killing them – the heathen Prussians in
particular – and eventually ruled all the land between the
Vistula and Memel from their string of rather fab castles. It's
almost funny, but, being Christians themselves, they were
nearly destroyed by Christian Polish and Lithuanian forces in
1410. The poor Teutonic Knights limped on until Napoleon
finally put paid to them, nicking all their remaining worldly
goods.

Odd Knights and Knightesses

Through the ages there have been all sorts of weird and
wonderful societies of knights including the Orders of Dog
and Cock, the Palm and Alligator, the Fools – no I'm not
making these up – the Bee, the Broom Flowers, the Slaves of
Virtue, the Angelic Knights, the Dove of Castile etc. as well
as a few female Orders.

KNIGHT KIT

One of the troubles with having pointy things like lances and swords stabbed at you, or sharp things like arrows and bolts fired at you, is that your skin isn't really designed for it. From the earliest of times men discovered that it might be a smart idea to put something tougher between their bodies and whatever it was that whomever it was was trying to puncture them with.

The trouble with wearing anything hard, unfortunately, is that it's usually inflexible and reduces the wearer's ability to run about (or away!). Something had to be found that was both bendy and tough at the same time. The answer was one of those things that seems obvious now – like the wheel (or the microchip, if you're a genius) – but was nothing less than inspired when first thought of.

Chain Mail

Until the end of the eleventh century, your average knight would go into battle dressed from head to knee in a sort of long, hooded frock (called a *hauberk*) made of little joined-up iron rings – like knitted metal. These rings would either be punched out of a sheet of iron or be handmade out of wire with the ends flattened. All in all there'd be upwards of a hundred thousand rings in your average garment, and the whole thing would weigh around 12 kilos. On top of the hood bit the knight would wear a conical (and

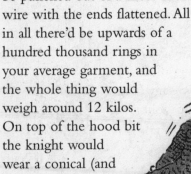

IS IT A LITTLE HEAVY DEAR?

sometimes comical) metal helmet or helm with a bit sticking down the front to protect his nose. For added protection he'd carry a huge shield shaped like a kite.

By the Way

The shield was made so big to enable a knight to carry a wounded mate on it if necessary.

Experts these days are continually astonished by the fact that, despite the European knights' contact with the heavily and cleverly armoured Turkish and Byzantine soldiers during the Crusades, hardly anything rubbed off on our boys. But it was from these infidels that English and French knights eventually nicked the idea of wearing a heavily padded and quilted undergarment (called a *gambeson*) underneath their chain mail, and a plain linen surcoat over it. They also pinched the concept of chain mail mittens and boots, which were laced on to the arms and legs.

By the twelfth century things had changed a lot. Instead of the pointy helmet that had replaced the conical sort, the knight went back to a cylindrical helmet, only this time much bigger (like a small upturned dustbin) which was so heavy that it was designed to rest on the wearers' shoulders. For the first time it covered the whole face, with slits for the eyes, and holes down the front for speaking (and presumably breathing). Later on these helms would sport ornaments – anything from plumes or fans to large scary horns – and could have movable visors. It being so cumbersome, any knight with any sense only put it on at the last minute.

By the Way

The cry 'helms on', was often the last cry heard before a medieval punch-up commenced. I expect 'run for it' could have been the second.

By Another Way

The trouble with the one-piece helmets was that, if the wearer received a blow, they could easily swivel round, moving the eye-slits away from the knight's vision and making him completely blind, which was a bit of a disadvantage in the old battle scenario.

Who's Who?

The next thing to happen was that the padded undergarment became lined with leather which had been boiled to make it harder. The linen surcoat began to carry an identifying coat of arms so that the soldiers knew who was who during a rumble, preventing the possibility of bashing or slashing someone on their own side. These identification symbols were the beginning of heraldry.

Proper Armour

The first proper plate armour was worn under the outergarments as extra protection (chilly or what?). Chain mittens only turned into gloves with fingers by the end of the twelfth century. By the beginning of the fourteenth century plates were appearing everywhere, protecting the front of the knees, shins, arms, elbows and shoulders. Mind you, a skilful swordsman could still find loads of places to poke his blade, like under the arms, in the neck or, dare I mention it, between the legs (ouch!). Later they developed little round steel discs called *basagews* purely to protect those vulnerable little places.

By the mid fourteenth century knights were beginning to look just how we imagine them now. They wore a fifty-fifty combination of mail and plate armour with a big sheet of shiny, shaped iron strapped over the chest. Covering this was a much shorter tunic tied at the sides called a tabard (the sort of thing dinnerladies wear)* with the knight's personal coat of arms on the front. As a knight's protection improved, by the way, so his shield got smaller . . . for fairly obvious reasons. So by now his shield wasn't much bigger than a tea tray.

Fully Tinned Up

This was about as far as it went for the English knights. They quite sensibly realised that there was a certain balance to be reached between protection and being able to run about – the more you had the less you could, so to speak! Otherwise you might just as well have been simply wheeled out in a great iron box with a hole for a spear or a sword in the front (mind you I've heard of worse ideas!).

* *Without the armour.*

The thick armour plate with pointed helmets and spikes on elbows and shoulders you see all those knights in pictures covered with from head to foot, was more than likely to have been made and worn by Italians, French or Germans and was often for purely ceremonial wear. The pig- or snout-faced helmets called *basinets* were designed to give the wearers a dead scary and dead hard appearance.

By the Way

Many fatalities were caused by the poor middle-aged knights dying of heart failure on the battlefield, before they even got near the enemy. If it happened to be a hot summer's day (especially likely in the Middle East), the poor guys could literally pot roast. This happened to Edward of York just before the Battle of Agincourt in France, though the temperature inside his suit probably owed a lot to his fatness as well.

The other slight problem that the armoured knight had to contend with occurred during thunderstorms – not from rust, as you might imagine, but from lightning. Many a knight and his horse were struck at the same time. At the battles of Crecy and Poitiers, more knights lost their lives from lightning strikes than from the best efforts of the enemy.

How Heavy?

It is widely believed that a full *harness*★ of armour was extremely heavy, to the point that the wearers could hardly move. But in the wonderful *Dictionary of Chivalry*, Grant Uden tells a different story. He suggests that the weight was all due to how well it was made. The finest armour fitted like a second skin and to achieve this armourers employed *hammer-men* to beat out the metal, *mill-men* to polish it up, and *locksmiths* to make all the bits and bobs like fastenings and hinges. If the blokes making the arms couldn't actually meet their customers (overseas battle commitments etc.), elaborate measurements or even actual models of their limbs were sent from far and wide.

Did you know, for instance, that:

1   A full harness in the fifteenth century was lighter than the full kit that foot soldiers had to wear in the First World War and the Household Cavalry wear these days?

★ *It's very uncool, apparently, if you ever meet a knight, to call it a 'suit' of armour.*

49

2   King Edward I (1239–1307) could leap into the saddle
     – without stirrups – in full armour, a bit like Red
     Indians did in the movies?

3   Tests in America recently showed that a fit young man
     in well-fitting armour these days could still run about
     quite athletically, jump on a horse and dismount
     without any help?

How Much?

If you are anything like me, you'll probably be more
interested in what all this gear cost. This is quite difficult to
find out, as many kings and landed gentry had their own
personal armourers. But the majority didn't, and would have
had to buy the stuff like anyone else. Not, however, off the
shelf, but specially tailored to fit their bodies – exactly.

A realistic figure, having spoken to various experts in the
field, is that a full set of armour, let alone anything you
might spend on horses and weapons, would probably set you
back the price of a new Ferrari (average about £150,000, in
case you don't have one). This, as you might imagine, really
would sort out the men from the boys.

Where?

As I said earlier, people like kings and dukes would probably have their own armourers situated in their castles. If you just wanted a one off set, however, you'd have to have them made at a private armourers. These were usually found in the East End of London around where Coleman Street is now. In 1322 anyone who wanted to make arms and armour had to belong to a guild and that guild, called the Armourers Company, is still going today.

By the Way

If you're after a new suit of armour, or a chain mail vest, or just a new sword – worry not. If you write to the Royal Armoury Museum in Leeds, they'll fix you up with something right away.

THINGS TO FIGHT WITH

Knights of old had a whole range of nasty things to hit and stab each other with. Here are a few of the best and also some of the weapons used by other people to hit and stab knights.

Battle-Axe
A nasty weapon if you happen to be on the receiving end. This would have a perfectly balanced handle around a metre and a half long and would be swung wildly round the head, using both hands. Knights often used the battle-axe in hand to hand conflict when knocked off their horses.

Dagger
More like a short sword; anything up to two feet long, double edged and sharp as a razor. The dagger began life (and also ended it!!) in the early Middle Ages.

Falchion
A type of sword used by knights and foot soldiers throughout the Middle Ages. Some widened considerably towards the point and had one convex cutting edge.

Fork
More popular with foot soldiers than knights, as they were often used to pull the knights off their horses. The fork had three ever so sharp prongs with hooks on the end to grip its object.

Glaive

A nasty looking weapon that was basically a curved sword stuck on the end of a long pole.

Guisarme

Again not popular with knights as they were used by foot soldiers to attack them. Guisarmes were a cross between a pike and a scythe – very unpleasant. Used in great swinging circles.

Halberd

A long-handled axe, sometimes six feet in length, with a nasty spike on the end. Often used like a can-opener against a fully tinned knight.

Lance

The main weapon of the knight both in battle and at jousts. For years it was simply a sharpened pole, over twelve feet in length, tipped with metal. Sometimes a special bracket was fitted to the breastplate of the armour so as to take the butt of the lance and therefore the impact. Later lances had a 'vamplate', a metal disc near the holding end specifically designed to protect the hands.

Mace

The most common sort of mace was the one with an iron ball on the end of a pole with sharp spikes sticking out all round. If one of these caught you you'd certainly know all about it, as it was capable of doing terrible damage. Some maces, called flails, were even more unpleasant. They had the spiky bit attached to a chain which was in turn attached to a handle. This meant that it could be swung round at great speed and could catch your opponent unawares.

Main-Gauche

From the French meaning *left-hand*. A nasty little dagger held in the left hand to parry blows while the other was busy with the big, proper sword.

Partisan

Another kind of halberd or pike, with a double-edged tapering blade on the end of a long pole. It was generally regarded as the knight's worst enemy.

Pole-Axe

Often used by knights, the six-foot long pole-axe did several jobs. It had a cutting edge, a hammerhead and a long spike on the end.

Rapier

Slim pointy sword used in hand to hand combat. Used to pierce the opponent rather than cut him.

Scimitar

Dangerous, single-edged, curved sword that broadened towards the point.

Two-Handed or Giant Sword

Massive sword that was so heavy it could only be held in two hands. Used in long sweeps this five to six feet long weapon could take a limb off (no trouble) – even if said limb was wearing armour.

War Hammer

Guaranteed to cause a bit of a headache if it caught your helmet, the war hammer looked a bit like the sort of hammer your dad uses but much bigger and on the end of a pole with a spike coming out of the top.

A KNIGHT'S HOME
IS HIS CASTLE

If you're wanting to know about knights, you'll probably
also need to know a bit about castles. I mean, you couldn't
really imagine a proud knight in full battle armour, astride a
magnificent charger pulling up outside a suburban semi –
he'd look a trifle silly (and, anyway, what would the
neighbours say!). Most English castles were built in those
rough, tough days around the twelfth century, when just
about everybody was fighting everybody. It became
necessary, therefore, for an English gentleman's home to be
built in such a style as to keep other English gentlemen out.
The peasants' homes, of course, didn't matter nearly so
much, as: a) nobody was really after theirs, and b) nobody
really gave a damn about what happened to peasants anyway.

Le Castle
The idea of castles as we know them really came from
France where the great lords had been knocking them up

for centuries. We know this because records show that back
in 864, that old smoothy Charles the Bald of France,
decreed, rather grumpily, that nobody could build one
without his say-so (so there!). This was a bit of a pain in the
derriére because castles were already part and parcel of the
feudal system, acting as the focal point of a knight's fief. In
return for the peasants sweating their guts out to feed and, if
picked, fight for the knight, the said knight had to provide a
great big safe house for them all to scurry back into if ever
they were being chased.

All Fall Down

Despite the fact that castles really began in France, it soon
became clear that the Norman masons who came over with
William the Conqueror weren't always that brilliant when
tall structures were required, and many of the great towers
they built over here simply fell down due to weedy
foundations. Actually this is not totally fair, because the poor
blokes only had Saxon labour to work with, and these early
Brits were rubbish at building anything bigger than a
park-keeper's hut.

Where?

Once a knight or baron had decided to build a new castle,
the next question had to be where to put the darn thing.
The answer was usually pretty obvious if you think about it
– on top of something – preferably a socking great hill. Not
only did this mean that your watchmen could see anyone
coming from miles around but also, if your new visitors
were slightly less than friendly, they'd usually be so
knackered by the time they reached the outer walls that they
couldn't do much anyway.

By the Way

By the middle of the eleventh century, castle builders decided that if there wasn't a natural hill near where they wanted it, they'd jolly well get the poor long-suffering peasants to make one, with their bare hands, and call it a *motte*. There are loads of these mottes, looking like overgrown molehills, all over England.

Castles were also usually built very close to rivers as this made the delivery of building materials (and water) much easier. There were very few roads around in those days (and those that there were, were usually Roman, clapped out, and seldom going anywhere near where you wanted to go!).

Made of What?

Once he had a site, Mr Knight had to decide what to build his castle out of. Just like the three little pigs found out to their cost, big bad wolves, or big bad enemies come to that, have little trouble attacking anything less substantial than stone. A couple of flaming arrows and the game was up – roast pork for all!

That's why none of the earlier castles, built out of wood, are still standing. But, despite all that, England in those days was mostly forest and so wood was free and there for the taking. In an attempt to get round the old fire problem, early timber-built castles often had really high, really wide, arrow-proof stone walls surrounding them.

What Sort of Castle?

There were two main types of castle in those days. Those with a *keep* – a big central building which could usually defend itself – and those without (which simply relied on the strength of the outer walls or palisades). Your top-of-the-range castle, of course, had both: a great big keep and huge surrounding walls and towers, within which all the other outbuildings were built. The keep, by the way, was where all the peasants ran to when there was trouble afoot.

One Way Out!

Early castles were usually built with only one entrance (and exit!) which was to prove rather silly, as it usually meant that relatively few attackers could simply hang around the front door as long as they liked, until the occupants just had to come out. Later castle designers got wise to this and made little concealed doorways (called posterns) round the back, so that if things got tricky the occupants could sneak away one at a time. Sometimes they even dug secret tunnels that came up in the fresh air as far away as they could be bothered to dig.

Most good castles would have a wide ditch or moat round them – the wider the better, filled with water (and, if possible, sharks)★. Those inside could lower and raise a drawbridge so that no one could get to them without a severe soaking.

Starting Off

First you had to get your peasant workers to start hauling up loads of timber or stones to the top of the hill they'd just

★ *Not really.*

made. These materials were often brought up-river on barges and unloaded as near as possible to the site. Castles usually had to be built in a hurry as knights (especially Norman knights) expected to be attacked by heathens every five minutes (which they often were). But what did these massive edifices cost? Well, if the records from 1296 of the building of Beaumaris Castle in Gwynedd, Wales, are anything to go by – an absolute fortune.

For a start, they had over a hundred carts and thirty boats running to and fro bringing the stone and also the wood (for the temporary buildings that the workmen had to live in). At the site itself were over 1,000 skilled carpenters, plasterers and stonemasons, as well as 2,000 minor workmen. All the time these men had to be protected from attackers and for this they employed ten watchmen, twenty crossbowmen and a hundred infantrymen. This building went on for thirteen years and was only half-finished when the top castle builder of the time, James of St George, died. Now I don't know about you, but that sounds pretty expensive to me. Mind you, that's nothing, Caernarvon castle, also in Wales, was started in 1283 and eventually finished (almost) in 1327 – forty-four years later.

By the Way

James was one of the most highly regarded architects and engineers of the time, earning the equivalent of £64,000 a year. Not much? If you consider what the poor labourers were being paid, it was a fortune.

Early Castles

In the very beginning, barons, their families, servants, pets and sometimes even farm animals all lived in one great and presumably rather niffy hall. When the Normans came, however, they weren't too keen on sharing with livestock (or was it the other way round?) and they moved the dirty beasts into the *bailey* (the bit between the main house and the outside wall). The boss and his family would then live on a raised *dais*, a paved floor just above the earth one. This main hall would be full of tables and benches, draped with animal skins and hung with curtains and colourful tapestries. The kitchen would usually be separate from the main hall, as cooking over massive open fires often led to stray sparks setting fire to the whole structure (which tended to ruin mealtimes). In the main hall the fire would be in the middle of the room, as far from the walls as possible (for obvious reasons). Smoke would escape through a little hole in the roof covered by its own little roof or louvre to stop the rain getting in.

Proper Castles

But what about those castles you see in picture books, with battlements and little pointy flags on the turrets? These began to appear, as I said earlier, in the twelfth century and many are still standing, admittedly a bit past their best, to this day. The inspiration for these wonderful buildings, particularly the pointy Gothic style, almost certainly came back with the Crusaders who had goggled at the fabulous fortresses and temples of the East (and had even brought back prisoners who knew how to build 'em).

THAT MIGHT CATCH ON

By the Way

One such prisoner, a bloke called *Lalys*, designed Neath Abbey and was Henry I's favourite architect.

By Another Way

Even if you want a simple garage built these days, your architect will probably have to knock out loads of boring technical drawings. These have to conform with local building regulations and the final plans will then have to be passed by the planning department of the local council before you can even lay the first brick. After said garage is finished, the building inspector will then have to come round and pass the work. In those days, because no drawings have ever been found, it seems pretty obvious that they simply scratched out what they wanted the thing to look like in the dust and promptly got on with it. Most of these castles then stood for hundreds of years. Does that tell us something?

The castle at Orford in Suffolk, which was started in 1165, is typical of many built at that time. Now derelict, it was originally located beside a harbour (which has since dried up). The main keep is circular inside but outside has three massive square towers protecting it and no doubt holding it up. Between these, on the outside, there were originally crenellated fighting decks.

There were storerooms and larders on the ground level and below them dungeons including the dreaded *oubliette* (from the French *oublier* – to forget), a hole in the ground into which the poor victim would be simply thrown and sort of – well – forgotten. Above the store rooms was a massive round main hall with beautifully painted beams soaring to a point high above the floor and above that would have been suites of rooms with a small kitchen for re-heating meals, making sauces and roasting and smoking small joints of meat. All the main cooking would have been done in the timber kitchens between the keep and the outer walls.

The bedrooms would have been set into the turrets adjoining the main structure (so the occupants could see out of the windows) and at the very top would have been a flat roof with the guards' quarters and watchtower. Just below would be a huge cistern that would have contained water for the whole castle. If you're wondering about lavs – yes, they did have them (after a fashion) but, not quite as good as those you have at home (I hope), they simply consisted of interconnecting chutes that ran from top to bottom, dropping down into a pit so deep that it would never have had to have been emptied. Better than nothing, I suppose.

Inside the average medieval castle's outer walls were usually loads of assorted buildings: chambers for the clergy, offices for the scribes and counting-houses for the castle's finance managers. There were wardrobes for the knight and his lady's clothes, dairies to make butter and cheese, carpentry shops for running repairs, aviaries for birds – both for singing and eating – and covered ways to keep the food dry as it was taken from the kitchen to the dining hall. There'd be a chapel to pray in, a safe room to keep all the gold and silver (and cash taken off the tenants) in, a special room in which to keep all the valuable deeds, an armoury for all the weapons, stables for the horses and a laundry for all the washing and ... pause for breath ... not forgetting, of course, wine cellars to keep the booze in, and a cool place for brewing beer. In fact it was like a small town within walls.

Approach With Caution

The main door at the front of the keep would have had a

gigantic portcullis (criss-cross barred gate) that could be raised and lowered from above. Just above the archway leading to this portcullis was usually a *murder hole* – a tricky, if somewhat obvious, device which was simply a hole in the ceiling through which rocks, arrows, hot oil, rotten eggs (or even worse!) could be deposited on unwanted visitors (like insurance salesmen) – brilliant stuff!

Breaking in

However fortified a castle might be, it didn't stop people trying to break in or beat the occupants into submission. One standard way of doing this was to dig underneath the castle with a view to undermining it. This happened at Rochester Castle way back in the twelfth century when the bad King John was laying siege to a bunch of knights he didn't quite see eye to eye with. He got his diggers to dig right under the south-east corner of the building and then stuff the tunnel with pit props and straw soaked in the fat of forty or so pigs (roast pork yet again). The huge fire caused the very foundations of the building to give way and brought down the massive corner turret. The king's men then rushed in and forced the rebels back into the keep, where, after eating all their horses, they eventually surrendered due to starvation.

This became such a common way of attacking a castle that the original builders eventually got wise to it and created a whole network of passages underneath so that they would soon be able to locate any new ones and shoo the interlopers away or smoke them out. Anyone with any real sense, however, built their castle on rock which solved the problem nicely.

By the Way

To get some idea of the scale of some of these operations, during the Mameluke attack on the fortress of Acre in 1291, a thousand engineers and miners attacked the eleven outer towers at the same time.

Over the Top

If this method didn't work, there were other ways of storming a castle. Best of all were the massive *war-machines*. The idea for these overgrown catapults called *mangonels* originally came from ancient Greece and they were powered by twisted animal skins and sinews that acted like whacking great elastic bands. There were also *ballistas*, giant crossbows which fired huge arrows or rocks horizontally. The rocks they fired would crack the outer surface of the castle walls allowing the attackers to tear away with picks and shovels at the rubble and loose stones that filled the two outer skins of your average castle wall. While they were doing this, of course, the defenders felt free to pour hot oil or tip rocks onto them – great fun. Eventually the workers got wise and wheeled in what was later called a *penthouse*, a portable wooden shelter under which they could beaver away to their hearts' content.

VERY FUNNY!

French Machines

Later, new stone-chucking machines from France, called *trebouchets*, were developed, powered by twisted skins and ultra-springy green wood. These worked by counterweight and were either small enough for one man to fire or so enormous (up to fifty feet in length) that it took over twenty men to operate and teams of oxen to get them into position. These were so big and powerful that they could've chucked a grand piano (if they'd had them). Both sides, in and out of the castle, would have these machines, and often the same missiles would be sent flying backwards and forwards time and time again.

By the Way

It was quite common to chuck the stinking carcasses of dead sheep or even horses over the walls in the hope of spreading disease amongst the inhabitants. Mean or what?

By Another Way

Attackers sometimes used *Greek fire*, a nasty mixture of naphtha, quicklime and sulphur which, when lit and catapulted in earthenware pots, would stick to whatever it came in contact with. This could be very unpleasant if that happened to be you. If thrown on water it would burn even more fiercely owing to the quicklime.

Gunsmoke

By the early fourteenth century everyone was talking about a new super-duper weapon, the idea for which was believed to have come from China. Early drawings show what look like a large vase tipped on its side with a massive arrow flying from its neck. At the back of the vase was a little armoured chap holding a lighted taper to a little hole. No prizes for guessing that this was an early cannon, powered by gunpowder, the recipe for which first appeared in England in a coded note by Roger Bacon, a monk, in 1260. It must be said, however, that despite the rather frightening banging of the early cannons, they were slow to load, had a short range and were no match for the skilled longbowmen in early battle trials.

Blow the Walls Down

If the assailants could reach the castle door or a flat piece of wall, they would use ginormous battering rams – huge tree trunks with metal ends, set into frames, mounted on rollers and covered in untreated (and smelly) animal skins to protect the *pushers* from being hit and set fire to by flaming missiles from above. Sometimes the defenders would lower straw mattresses to cushion the blows from the ram or huge hooks on chains to try to pull the dreadful thing out of the way.

Siege Towers

As well as huge ladders for scaling the walls, the attackers would knock up lofty towers the same height as the walls. They would then flatten the land up to the walls and wheel them into place so that the soldiers could throw bridges across onto the battlements. The towers, often several storeys high, would usually be covered in waterlogged animal skins to ward off attacks by flaming arrows.

Siege Time

All that tunnelling and shooting and ramming and stuff was all very well, but it often seemed like very hard work, and rather unnecessary. It was much easier to just surround a castle, with said knight and his company locked safely inside, cut off all their supplies and communications and simply sit it out. King Stephen (1135–54) in fact spent most of his reign lounging around outside one castle or another waiting for the people inside to come out with their hands up. These sieges could go on for months or, on rare occasions, years, only ending when those inside had eaten just about everything possible to eat (including each other) and drunk everything possible to drink (yes, even that!!!). Sometimes, if a well ran dry, or the water supply was cut off, the inmates would resort to drinking the vast wine supplies that castles usually kept in the cellars. They not only drank it, but used it to cook and even, when really desperate, put out fires with it, which, as a lover of the grape, seems a dreadful waste to me.

Food Alert!

The famous siege of Rouen by our Henry V went on from 29th July 1418 to 13th January 1419. By Christmas the inhabitants had run out of food completely and, having eaten all their supplies, were down to horses, dogs, cats, mice (and old-age pensioners) with the occasional rat for afters. So as not to appear to be giving in, those who could still stand upright were paraded along the battlements to try to make the English think that everything was still OK. Some of the poorer townsfolk however, men, women and children, were shoved outside the town gates and told they had to fend for themselves. It was then that the real picture was revealed. It was the old good news and bad news scenario yet again. Sure our kind king took pity on them and gave them food and water but unfortunately he wouldn't have them in his camp so most died from the freezing cold and damp.

Most of the time those doing the sieging would have quite a pleasant break, waiting around for those inside to give in, and it was not unknown to have feasts and tournaments to pass the time. Sometimes, however, those outside had real trouble getting food and supplies themselves. This could be a problem especially if those inside had realised that they were due for a siege at some time or another, and had had the good sense to stock up. It was not unusual, therefore, to have a scenario where the siegers, starving to death, threw up their hands in submission and sloped off home.

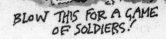

BLOW THIS FOR A GAME OF SOLDIERS!

End Note

Towards the end of the Middle Ages most people were beginning to behave themselves, so the need for massive stone-built fortifications, towers and moats was considerably reduced. The age of the castle was soon to be over.

TOURNAMENTS

If we reckon knights liked hunting, feasting, and breaking into each other's castles, they liked tournaments even more. Nothing was better designed to show off what they were all about than these elaborate medieval festivals (apart from maybe Crusades). A young knight could display bravery, agility, mercy and fair play while seeking employment with the lords who were always on the lookout, like football scouts, for new talent. Not only that, but it was a way for a poor man to make a fortune and gain lands and respect. Best of all, it was a chance to show off in front of the local babes and compete for their favours.

By the Way
Some of the prizes were truly wonderful but, as I'll explain a bit later, the knights could end up being the prizes themselves.

If hunting was unpopular with the Church, tournaments were the ultimate no-no as they were seen as just a lightly hidden training ground for war. 'An execrable and accursed game' (as some religious bloke called it). Even Henry II forbade them because of the shocking waste of young lives. And shocking it often was: William Marshal, a knight who fought twice a month when young, claimed that in 1240 between sixty and eighty contestants were slaughtered in a frenzy of killing – at one single tournament.

By the Way
After one famous victory poor Will had to resort to the blacksmith's shop to have his head prised out of his helmet.

HE REALLY SHOULD KEEP HIS HELMET ON!

King Richard the Lionheart (1157–99) wasn't nearly so worried about the loss of life, seeing it as a way of drumming up money for his Crusades. He licensed five sites called *steads* for them to take place. In order to take part a combatant had to pay a fee in advance according to rank. Earls would pay twenty marks, and a poor knight with no land would only have to pay two.

That was in the early days, however, when tournaments were not much less than free-for-alls with posses of knights from various towns or cities attacking each other in fearsome battles. The object was usually to take as many prisoners as possible and ransom them back to their families.

All for One

As tournaments developed, they became less like brawls between rival gangs and more like individual campaigns for aspiring young knights. In fact these guys would wander the countryside, like prizefighters or even gunslingers looking for tournaments to not only show off their skills at, but in order to earn huge amounts of cash and maybe even get their chain-mailed mits on the lord's prettiest daughter. Some knights became completely addicted to tournaments, mortgaging their estates and livestock even when it led to eventual bankruptcy and ruin. Sure the big prize could set you up for life, but if you lost (and provided you weren't killed) you could expect to lose your horse, your armour and if really unlucky, your freedom. Individual knights, beaten fairly and squarely in battle, often ended up being ransomed by their victor – can you imagine?

Despite all the vibrant colour and music and feasting and carnival atmosphere, however, tournaments were still basically savage affairs with healthy young warriors often ending their days bleeding to death on the grass in front of a rapturous audience, a bit like gladiators in Roman times (except then it was sand not grass!).

Going Soft

Later on, in an effort to curb the fatalities, weapons were blunted and barriers were put between the jousters to stop them crashing into one another. Even so, when tournaments had become merely stylised parodies of themselves, the odd lance could still penetrate the odd visor and give the occupant quite a bit more than a headache. More than that, if tempers got lost, no amount of blunting of weapons could save the combatants from doing each other in. At one tournament at Chalons in 1273 the Duke of Burgundy really lost it and seized our very own King Edward I round the neck in an attempt to pull him off his horse and strangle him. Our Eddie didn't go for this and galloped off dangling the desperate Duke behind him. Suddenly foot soldiers on both sides dashed to support their leaders and both sides fired their crossbows at each other – good game! Many people were killed at what became *The Battle of Chalons*.

Trouble at Home

All this tournamenting was very well but it often led to the knights neglecting their lands back home and at one stage it became difficult for a king to raise an army to go and kill his enemies with, as there were so many knights busy killing each other – for fun.

Later Tournaments

Towards the end of the Middle Ages, tournaments changed
from being bloody battlegrounds to rather theatrical displays
of wealth, breeding and athletic skills. Impoverished knights
from not very good families found it impossible to get a
look-in, for the cost of armour and all the kit that went
with taking part (horses etc.) was becoming silly. Hand-to-
hand fighting to the death became practically a thing of the
past and jousting, with all the new safety rules and
regulations, became top of the bill.

Scoring was down to how many
times a knight struck his
opponent and where. A blow
to the helmet was top
target, but if he actually
managed to knock his
opponent off his horse
he'd hit the jackpot
big time.

Costs

So what did it all cost? Answer – one helluva lot! One
knight, who went by the name of William de la Zouche
paid well over the equivalent of £32,000 pounds to King
Edward III's armourer John Skelton simply for gold and
silver foil, silk fringes and all the bits and pieces that went
into decorating the harnesses, banners, crests and fabrics for
himself and his horse. That was without his actual armour,
the cost of which I've already given you some idea of.

GOOD KNIGHTS

Though most of the knights of the Middle Ages received a bad press, others became famous for their heroism and bravery. Here are my favourites.

Salah ad-Din

Salah ad-Din (1137–1193) – Saladin for short – was the sultan of all Egypt and Syria, which was a pretty big job. He was also the head infidel and most famous of all the Saracen chiefs. On top of this he was the most feared enemy of the Crusaders. Saladin, a small, modest, scholarly man was obviously not a proper knight, but most reporters of the time claimed he had most of the knightly qualities that so many of the so-called Christians lacked. He was known for amazing acts of generosity and true chivalry.

Once when under negotiations with our flamboyant, over-the-top Richard the Lionheart, about who was to rule Ascalon, he heard that Richard was dying with the dreaded fever in his tent. He then sent fresh peaches and pears and even snow from the peak of Mount Hermon to help cool him down. Another time, when Richard had parted company with his horse in battle, he sent him a few more. Poor Saladin died when only fifty-four, worn out by continual fighting.

Sir William Longsword

Another knight who, at only twenty-seven, was more famous for his spectacular death at Massoura, Egypt, than anything else. In 1250 the Christian knights were getting a right pasting from the Egyptian infidel army. It had come down to hand-to-hand fighting in the streets of the city and the brave Sir William with his standard-bearer Sir Richard de Guise were getting the worst of it. Richard had already lost his hand and was doing the best he could to hold the banner up with his brand new stump. Then the Saracens, who couldn't seem to get our Sir William out of his saddle, sliced off his left foot. This annoyed the young knight, so he got down from the saddle and, supporting himself on another mate, Richard de Ascalon, carried on fighting on the other leg. Then another sword swipe took care of his right arm, which was inconvenient, to say the least. Now without any support at all, he hopped into the attack once more, grasping his sword in his other hand which was promptly lopped off too, by yet another Saracen blow. Oh dear, things were now looking pretty tricky for our poor handless, armless and one-footed warrior and it wasn't long before he tripped over and was set upon by the Saracen swordsmen until there was hardly anything recognisable left of poor Willie. Whilst this was happening, Richard de Ascalon had fallen upon his master to try to save him but, as you might imagine, he suffered the same fate.

Sir Giles d'Argentine

Probably the most famous knight to feature in the battle of Bannockburn (1314) at which the English were shown where to get off by Robert the Bruce. (What is a Bruce?). With the archers cut into little pieces and the cavalry up to their necks in the peat bogs, the English king was dragged from the fun by a company of his

most trusty knights, who then galloped off with him towards
Stirling and safety. After they were out of harm's reach, the
brave (if not stupid) Sir Giles pulled up his horse and cried,
'I am not of custom to fly; nor shall I do so now. God keep
you!' With that he charged back towards the battle and
certain death. Silly man!

John FitzThomas, Earl of Kildare

One of Edward I's knights during the Scottish wars always
carried the livery of a chained monkey on his crest.
Apparently, one night, when he was a little nipper in the
Castle of Woodstock, Ireland, a really bad fire broke out. So
bad that with all the rushing around no one thought to get
little Johnny until it seemed too late. So it was, for at the end
of the night, when they finally got to the poor little mite's
bedroom it was burned to cinders. The end of the knight?
No . . . just as they were tearing their hair out with grief,
they heard a strange noise
coming from high on
the battlements. It
was the family's pet
monkey (who was
usually chained up),
with the tiny babe in its
arms. When he grew up
and became a knight (the
baby not the monkey) Sir
John put the monkey on his
crest in gratitude.

Sir James Douglas the Good

After the death of King Robert the Bruce in 1329, Scottish
knight Sir Douglas was given his leader's heart in a silver

casket. He was asked to take it to the Holy Land, so that Bruce could be seen to carry out his Crusader's vow (to lead the army to get the Holy Land back for the Christians).

While he was travelling through Spain he couldn't resist joining the King of Castile who was about to have a rumble with the Moors of Granada. Bad move. He was soon dying from horrid wounds and rather perturbed that he couldn't carry out his master's wishes. Without further ado he lobbed the dead boss's ticker right into the heart of the battle crying, 'Go first as thou wert want to go'.

Luckily (if you're into dead hearts) someone found the blinking thing after the soldiers had all gone home and brought it back to Scotland.

Sir Howel-y-Fwyall

Young Welsh soldier Howel did so well swinging his pole-axe while fighting with the Black Prince at Poitiers that the prince made him a knight and awarded him what was rather horribly referred to as a 'mess of meat' to be served to him every night (a good job he wasn't a veggie). When he died, the mess was given to the poor instead.

Thomas Holland

If you're going to capture someone make sure they've got a few quid. Thomas Holland, a young impoverished knight, captured and ransomed the ludicrously wealthy Count Eu at the storming of Caen, France, in 1346. This, as you might imagine, made him a very rich man. Just to make it the perfect storybook ending, he married a princess called Joan the Fair Maid of Kent, said to have been the most beautiful woman of the age, and became an earl. Don't some people make you sick? If it's any consolation, he didn't, apparently, live happily ever after.

Sir John Chandos

Probably the most celebrated knight on the battle circuits of the Middle Ages, Sir John became a Knight of the Garter three years after the Battle of Crecy and in 1356 fought beside the Black Prince at Poitiers. Despite his wonderful record of bravery on the battlefield, poor old John was more famous for the way he died.

One day while just about to commence a battle at Mortemer in 1370, he strode out surrounded by his men to face the enemy. Sir John had a habit of wearing a huge cloak carrying his coat of arms and it was this that caused his downfall (or falldown). As he was approaching the enemy line, sword in hand, a gust of wind blew the cloak round his legs and he began to trip forward, breaking into a short run to correct himself. One of his foes, a squire called James St Martin, who was to his right, shoved out his lance on the off-chance. Normally Sir John would have easily ducked out of the way but, as luck would have it, he'd lost his right eye in a hunting accident five years earlier and saw nothing. Added to that he hadn't had time to pull his visor down. As it happened, the lance went in exactly where his right eye should have been, so he'd have lost it again anyway (if he hadn't died the following day).

John, Sixth Earl of Ormonde

An Irish nobleman of whom Edward IV said 'if good breeding and liberal qualities were lost in the world, they might all be found in the Earl of Ormonde.'

In 1449 the bailiff of Evreaux (small town in North-West France) was sent with a bunch of soldiers to order the good people of Vernon (another small town in North-West France) to give themselves up to the King of France and to send him the keys of the town. John Ormonde, who was governing the town for the English, thought he'd have a bit of a laugh and sent every key he could lay his hands on. The bailiff didn't get the joke and soon the town was under attack. Ormonde got an arrow right through both cheeks (see *Bad reactions to jokes in ancient history*). The two sides decided to talk, which must have been a trifle difficult for poor John, but eventually all the 250 English were allowed to leave with their suitcases, provided the French agreed to tell the King that the surrender had nothing to do with them.

BAD KNIGHTS

Most of us like to think of knights, as I said in the intro, as fine, noble gentlemen fighting for their king and country. This was sometimes true, but it was only a fraction of the story. Many knights, I'm afraid, were cruel, dishonest, self-seeking ba...ba...*barbarians*.

In fact, long before the First Crusade, the Byzantine Emperor Alexius, whom the Christian knights were supposed to be on their way to Constantinople to help, was very wary of these approaching Westerners. He regarded them as fickle and savage and mostly spoiling for a fight when sometimes a helpful chat would have done just as well. Alexius only had to hear the reports of how these knights carried on back home in their own backyards (when not out robbing and pillaging their neighbours) to realise what an uncivilised bunch most of them were.

English Jungle

He saw English life like the jungle, where both predator and/or victim snarled in their various castle lairs, hanging around eating and drinking to excess, while working out not only whom they could vanquish or oppress but who the people who'd next try to do it to them were. These knights terrorised the common folk, embarrassed the church and were a continual threat to the King.

The noble rank of knight had more or less devoted itself to warfare. While the knights' labouring serfs toiled in the fields, the knights simply hung around their castle keeps in jaded luxury, dying for the chance to polish up their weapons, saddle up their warhorses, pull their squires out of bed, don the old armour, say farewell to the missis, gather their mates and soldiers and get out on the road looking for action.

For your average knight, the perfect day out would be to breach a neighbouring castle's walls, hear the clash of steel on steel and the screams for help from the wounded in agony, witness riderless horses idly munching the bloodsoaked grass and survey fields scattered with dead soldiers peppered with arrows and pinned to the ground by broken lances. As far as he was concerned, this all glorified war as man's highest achievement. Not for the feudal knight all that boring stuff like growing things or building things, or making people better or praying for their souls. Oh, no! Knights embraced war and fighting with a passion.

Best of all, the more a knight carried on like that, in dear old Merrie Medieval England, the more honour and praise seemed to be heaped on him. The medieval knight became akin to a mini-dictator, king of his own domain, ungovernable and not answerable to anyone.

An Englishman's Home
The very worst period of all came after the arrival of the mild-mannered King Stephen to the throne (reigned

1135–1154). All the knights and barons, seeing his weakness, took advantage and any form of law and order was completely forgotten. Hundreds of illegal castles were planned and the wicked men who wanted to build them would scour the countryside capturing any poor peasant they came across. These poor devils were made to work on the castle building and when finished they'd be forced into virtual slavery as the master's servants. Any whom they thought might have any money were thrown into squalid dungeons and tortured until they gave it up. Some were hung up by their thumbs and smoked like kippers, some had burning things tied to their feet, while some had ropes twisted round their heads till their very skulls split and their brains exploded. Some were thrown into dungeons full of nasty poisonous snakes and slimy toads, while others were crushed into small chests (called *crucet-houses*) which were then filled with sharp, heavy stones till all their arms and legs were broken. Rather popular was the use of spiked steel collars that made it impossible for the poor wearer to lie down or sleep.

These naughty knights squeezed protection money from the impoverished villagers, until, when their meagre savings ran out, their villages were burnt to the ground. Eventually there wasn't an occupied village to be found in areas like the Fenlands and there was no food to be had for love nor money. Throughout the land the feudal knight became simply a force for evil.

It wasn't much better over in the land of the Franks (France), so when the idea of a holy war cropped up, there was always a rush of people trying to escape the famine, constant civil wars and an agonising new fever called St Anthony's Fire.

Geoffrey de Mandeville

Right at the top of the noxious knight league was a bloke called Geoffrey de Mandeville of Ely, Norfolk. He ran his estate down so much that for thirty miles round his castle not an ox nor a plough could be seen and the price of grain soared to 200 pennies a bushel. The poor folk died in their droves from starvation and lay about in the fields to be pecked by the crows and torn apart by the beasts of the field (hedgehogs, bunnies etc.). Those that survived were tortured mercilessly for any money they might have.

Mind You

Geoff de Mandeville got his come-uppance. He was trampled to death at a tournament. Ha ha!

Simon de Montfort

Not our English one – otherwise known as the Earl of Leicester – this French Simon de Montfort was a Norman knight who led the Crusade on behalf of his countrymen. He ordered that whenever a castle was taken by force, everyone inside should be massacred – no questions asked. For years he waged war against the powerful religious and anti-Catholic sect the Cathars (who didn't believe in Jesus but did believe that Man was created by the Devil). At Minerve he took 140 of their black-robed priests and flung them onto a bonfire. At Lavaur 400 were also burnt and their defenders, Aimery de Montreal and eighty of his

knights, were hanged. The famous
lady-priest Giraude de Laurac was
flung down a well and rocks were
thrown down on top of her in case
she got too comfortable. De
Montfort was finally killed himself
by a huge stone thrown from the
battlements of Toulouse by one of
the women defending it – 'the stone
flew to its proper mark, and smote
Count Simon on his steel helm so
that his eyeballs, brains, teeth and
skull all flew into pieces'. Served
him right too, says I.

Bohemund of Taranto

A famous Norman Crusader who was strictly in it for the
money. Bohemund was a tall, hugely built, spectacularly
handsome man with oodles of charm. But he was moody
and very resentful of people who were better off than him
(which was just about everyone). While chasing the Turkish
Muslims through Syria, his army of knights began to despair
through lack of food and had to sell all their armour and
weapons to survive. To cheer his knights up, Bohemund
roasted all their donkeys and then the Muslim captives (but I
don't know if they ate them too). Bohemund was one of
those generals in charge of the siege of Nicaea (page 30) and
it was probably his idea to catapult the heads of his Muslim
captives over the wall. Nice bloke!

Count Emmich of Leisingen

A German knight who gathered a sizeable army of
Crusaders in the Rhineland, Germany. Just as they were

about to set out for the Holy Land, someone asked him why they were going all that way to fight the enemies of Christianity, when the very people who'd crucified Jesus, the Jews, were all around them living in just about every European city. Good point, said the cocky count, and promptly marched on the city of Worms where a lot of Jewish people were living. The Bishop of Worms, fearing trouble, let them into his palace to shelter, but Emmich and his army broke in and slaughtered 500 men, women and children. When Crusaders reached the German town of Mainz, the Jewish community tried to buy him and his murderous mates off with as much gold as they could muster, which the greedy count gratefully accepted. The next day Emmich ordered his men to slaughter the lot of them (over 1,000) anyway. From then on no Jew was safe from being murdered, all under the excuse that Emmich and his men were carrying out God's revenge for the loss of His Son.

Baldwin of Bouillon

Baldwin set out on the Crusades with his brothers Godfrey and Eustace, the red crosses emblazoned on their white leather tunics. Unlike his blond, handsome and charming brothers, Baldwin was dark, cold and mean-looking. He was supposed to have gone into the Church but Baldwin was after luxury and women. When he left for the Crusades he took his wife and kids with him and was determined to grab some land and treasure for his trouble – he didn't care a fig for God. The stories of his cruelty are legendary. Once, while on the way to the Holy Land, he managed to become master of the city of Tarsus, having cheated his mate Tancred, who'd originally captured it off the infidels, out of it. He was supposed to hand it over to the Byzantine Emperor Alexius as part of the whole Crusader's deal but had no intention of doing so. When a bunch of 300 Norman Knights turned up to help defend the city he wouldn't let 'em in, saying that they should carry on marching. The poor tired Normans were forced to sleep outside the city walls. The infidels (who hadn't really gone away) massacred them to a man. A few weeks later Baldwin decided he didn't want the city much after all, so he simply deserted, leaving it to a bunch of pirates.

Either way, God didn't seem to mind, for the horrible Baldwin eventually became King of Jerusalem in 1100 having set out on the Crusades as a penniless adventurer.

Richard the Lionheart

You might be surprised to find Richard in this chapter. After all, wasn't he supposed to be one of the most dashing heroes England ever produced? True he was tall, immensely strong, blond, charming and so handsome that friends and enemies alike fell under his spell. But that was the good side. The other was far more dubious. Richard had a foul temper, which came out whenever he didn't get his way.

His cruelty knew no bounds. In 1177 he crushed a French revolt at Barbeziex. He ended up with 2,500 prisoners and couldn't make up his mind exactly how to teach 'em a lesson. He eventually decided on three solutions. The first third he beheaded in front of all the others. The second third he had drowned in the river in front of the last third. He then blinded the remainder and left them staggering around with orders to proclaim the king's justice to whomever they met.

THE END OF THE KNIGHT

By the end of the thirteenth century the whole knight
business was in a pretty sorry state, as most had blown their
money on crusading or tournaments. Almost unbelievably,
the actual rank of knighthood, that most noble symbol of
Englishdom, was up for sale on the open market, like a
pound of sprouts or a Jersey cow. The prob was that nobody
with half a grain of sense wanted to be a knight anymore –
it was too damned expensive. For a start, armour was
becoming more and more complex, robust (and thick) in
order to keep out bolts from the new-fangled crossbow, and
it doesn't take a degree in economics to work out that this
was reflected in the price. Then there was the dear old
warhorse. These big brutes (they often had to have several)
cost maybe twenty times as much as an ordinary horse – and
to protect their master's investment they needed armour too.
Then there was the cost of equipping a small bunch of men
to fight for the knight's overlord. All in all your poor knight
was having to spend nearly all his cash on this – and he
didn't like it much. He'd much prefer to stay home and look
after his estate. Who can blame him?

Compulsory Knights
It got so bad that Edward I ordered that anyone who had
freehold lands bringing in more than twenty quid a year,
had to become a knight – or else pay a large fine to cover
the cost of hiring mercenaries. Many English gentlemen
willingly paid this fine so's not to go broke but alas, some
knights became virtual beggars, forced to go to
moneylenders or plead with rich townsfolk to survive.

So all that chivalry, like devotion to his faith and his lord, and all that vowing to be a defender of women, children and the sick, went right out of the castle window as the boot became firmly placed on the other foot.

Instead of protecting their peasants, some knights now preyed on them, making them work for no money, taking whatever they owned and giving nothing in return. English knights had also lost what they found most precious – respect on the battlefields of Europe. All they were after now was hard cash in the form of ransoms. A dead foe was no use to a broke knight, but a live one could be sold back to his lord or family for a castle full of dosh.

Soldiers for Hire

Often savage and unprincipled mercenaries had to be found to fight battles, if the knights refused to do it. These guys were simply hired killers who murdered and robbed for anyone who'd pay them enough loot.

Something had to be done, so Edward eventually reintroduced conscription, which meant that every able-bodied man of a certain age was forced to fight for his country. Oddly enough, this actually worked a treat. By the time of the Hundred Years War with France in the fourteenth and fifteenth centuries, Edward III had a huge army of well-trained soldiers fighting for their king and country once more. For the first time since the age of chivalry had begun, all men, rather than just a particular class, were willing to go to war for land and glory . . . and their King.

Knightfall

Meanwhile, with the introduction of new weapons, such as
the longbow, the heavily armoured knight had had his day.
At the Battle of Crecy (1346), in which the English
longbowmen massacred the French crossbowmen, cruel
English foot-soldiers ran amongst the armoured, unsaddled
French knights lying winded and helpless in the mud. They
rammed their long daggers deep into the eye slits of their
helmets killing them instantly. Who says the English were
always gentlemen? (Actually, these guys turned out to be
Welsh, but we won't go into that now.) All in all, 1,542
French knights and lords were slain while we only lost two.
That's what I call a result.

By the Way

A well-fired arrow from an English longbow could pierce
chain mail, a four-inch oak door or bring a horse down
from a range of 180 metres. One of
William de Braose's knights was
unlucky enough to be on the
receiving end of an arrow that went
straight through the skirts of his
mail shirt, through his mail
trousers, through his thigh, and
through the wooden bit of his
saddle until it finally came to
rest pinning him to his poor
old horse's bum.

Knights for All

Eventually, quite ordinary people, like rich townsfolk, were made knights, but, unlike these days, when only the Queen can do it, anyone who was a knight could make anyone who wasn't a knight . . . a knight. The whole thing began to get out of hand, with your average knight making knights out of people he either liked or simply owed money to. He could even turn his little kids into knights before they even knew what the word meant – and they wouldn't have to make vows, or serve any sort of apprenticeship. It was a complete free-for-all – a joke.

These days, as we all know, even ageing pop stars, retired footballers and failed politicians get made into knights or even lords, so I suppose we can safely say that the idea of your knight as a noble, God-fearing symbol of English nobility, ready to fight in foreign lands for the honour of his country and God has really disappeared down the proverbial pan. Shame really!

THE SHORT AND BLOODY HISTORY OF

All aboard, Landlubbers!

PIRATES

John Farman

Have you ever wondered why pirates wore gold earrings, or where the saying 'sick as a parrot' came from? And do you know who the cruellest pirate in history was?

John Farman's got all the answers, so come aboard for his short and bloody history of the day-to-day life of pirates!

£3.99   0 09 940709 4

THE SHORT AND

BLOODY

HISTORY

OF

Call me Inspector!

SPIES

John Farman

Psst! Do you know how to make invisible
ink or send a coded message? And have
you heard about the pope who was a spy?
John Farman's been doing some spying of his
own and has uncovered all the answers in this
fantastic book. But beware, this message will
self-destruct in five seconds!

£3.99   0 09 940715 9

THE SHORT AND
BLOODY
HISTORY
OF

Fancy a joust?

KNIGHTS

John Farman

Have you ever wondered how knights managed to walk, let alone fight, covered from head to foot in metal? And have you heard about the knights who became addicted to jousting? Or the one who was rescued by a monkey? It's all in John Farman's brilliant book. So arm yourself for a fact attack!

£3.99   0 09 940712

THE VERY BLOODY HISTORY of BRITAIN

PART 1

&

THE VERY BLOODY HISTORY of BRITAIN

1945 TO NOW

WITHOUT THE BORING BITS

AND STILL NOT BORING!

Warning!!! These books could change your ideas about history for ever!

By John Farman

Do you know...
WHO planned the first Channel tunnel?
WHEN 10 Downing Street was built?
WHY there were vampires in Britain?

Bizarre, barmy and almost beyond belief, John Farman's
THE VERY BLOODY HISTORY books make boring
history lessons a thing of the – er – past.

John Farman
THE VERY BLOODY HISTORY OF BRITAIN PART 1
Red Fox paperback £3.99 ISBN 0 09 984010 3

THE VERY BLOODY HISTORY OF BRITAIN – 1945 to now
Red Fox paperback £3.99 ISBN 0 09 937221 5

The Very Bloody History of London

By John Farman

WITHOUT THE BORING BITS

When a man is tired of London, he is tired of life... **Samuel Johnson**

Let John Farman, author of the mega-bestselling title *The Very Bloody History of Britain,* guide you round one of the world's most famous cities, London. Packed with a multitude of facts to entertain and amaze you, *The Very Bloody History of London* will take you on a tour you will never forget. Sometimes grisly, but always fascinating, this is history as it should be – loads of fun!

John Farman
THE VERY BLOODY HISTORY OF LONDON
Red Fox paperback, £3.99, ISBN 0 09 940412 5